Chatting in Idiomatic English

*Challenges
for Advancing
ESL Learners*

by Anne Simeon

BENDALL BOOKS
Educational Publishers

BENDALL BOOKS
Educational Publishers
CANADIAN ADDRESS: P.O. Box 115, Mill Bay, B.C. V0R 2P0
U.S. ADDRESS: 1574 Gulf Road, Unit 361, Point Roberts, WA 98281
ELECTRONIC MAIL: bendallbooks@islandnet.com
WORLD WIDE WEB URL: http://www.islandnet.com/bendallbooks

CHATTING IN IDIOMATIC ENGLISH
Copyright © 1995 by Anne Simeon. All rights reserved.

CANADIAN CATALOGUING IN PUBLICATION DATA

Simeon, Anne, 1911-
   Chatting in idiomatic English

   ISBN 0-9696985-1-8
   1. English language—Textbooks for second language learners.*
2. English language—Idioms. 3. Figures of speech. I. Title.
PE1128.S55 1995   428.3'4   C95-910284-1

Printed in Canada
 96 97 98 5 4 3 2

Contents

Chatting in Idiomatic English

Written for upper-intermediate and advanced English as a Second Language students, these twelve chats are designed to make idioms fun to learn in their proper context. The meanings of the idioms follow each of the chats.

Turning A Deaf Ear 1

Second Thoughts 5

Ripped Off! 9

A Sight For The Gods 13

Where There's A Will There's A Way 17

Father And Son 21

Throwing In The Towel 25

No Accounting For Taste 29

No Huskies For Ted 33

A Mother And Daughter At Odds 37

A Change For The Better 41

In The Money 45

Turning A Deaf Ear

Sue: Hello, Auntie. I'm on top of the world today. Rob and I are going to get hitched next month.

Aunt: Oh Sue, I hate to pour cold water on your happiness, but I've been hearing about your new heart throb and I hope you will think carefully about marrying a sixty-four year old, penniless artist. Apart from his age, his reputation is nothing to write home about.

Sue: Who've you been talking to?

Aunt: Someone at the art gallery. Rob did odd jobs there once. He was always late for work and is suspected of having been light-fingered. He left under a cloud.

Sue: The fellow you spoke to is talking through his hat. Rob left that job because he couldn't hack getting up early to go to work. That's no sin. I thought you would be thrilled to hear my wonderful news.

Aunt: Oh, I'm so sorry, dear. I just want to see you happily married and I can't believe you will be happy with someone like Rob. You must know that he pinched some paints from an art shop last year and was caught red-handed. He spent time in the slammer, didn't he?

Sue: That's water under the bridge. Rob was in the doldrums at the time and needed paints to finish a masterpiece. One can't make an omelet without breaking eggs, you know. He intends to give the store a painting sometime to pay for the stuff he took. Fair exchange is not robbery.

Aunt: That depends... How much do his paintings sell for?

Sue: He hasn't sold any yet, but no problem. One day Rob's work will take the world by storm, and then our life'll be a piece of cake.

Aunt: Things don't always pan out as hoped. Forgive me, dear, but I can't see your life being the bed of roses you imagine. What do your parents think?

Sue: Well, they do take a dim view of my engagement. For one thing, they say that Rob's too old for me. I know he's sixty-four, but that doesn't mean he's not full of get up and go.

Aunt: Rob's no spring chicken, that's for sure. He's too long in the tooth for a young girl like you. For that reason, I consider him a poor match for my favourite niece.

Sue: Auntie, I do wish you wouldn't talk like that when I'm on cloud nine and can't wait to be Rob's second half. You must admit that I'm old enough to paddle my own canoe.

Aunt: Of course you are, dear. I'll pipe down right now and wish you every happiness.

Turning A Deaf Ear — Idioms

Be on top of the world	Be very happy
Get hitched	Get married
Pour cold water on	Say something to spoil a person's happiness, etc.
Heart throb	Person one is in love with
Nothing to write home about	Nothing good enough to write about
Light-fingered	Liable to steal
Leave under a cloud	Leave in disfavour
Talk through his hat	Talk nonsense
Can't hack it	Finds it too difficult
To pinch	To steal
Catch red-handed	Catch in the act of doing
In the slammer	In jail
Water under the bridge	Over, finished
Be in the doldrums	Be in a state of lacking money, job, inspiration

Can't make an omelet without breaking eggs	Nothing can be made without the proper materials
Fair exchange is no robbery	(Meaning is obvious)
Take the world by storm	Make a great impression
Piece of cake	Very easy and pleasant
To pan out	To come up to expectations
Bed of roses	Very happy situation
A dim view	Very poor opinion
Full of get up and go	Energetic, youthful
No spring chicken	Not young
Long in the tooth	Old
Be on cloud nine	Be very happy
Second half	Spouse
Paddle own canoe	(Meaning is obvious)
To pipe down	To stop talking

Second Thoughts

Tom: How are you and Marilyn planning to celebrate your golden handshake next year?

Alan: We haven't decided yet. A Caribbean cruise is in the cards. Unfortunately, Marilyn is a very bad sailor, and feeds the fish even in the calmest weather.

Tom: That's too bad. No wonder you're hesitant about a cruise.

Alan: Well, Marilyn is willing to give cruising a whirl, but I must admit that something I heard on the news this morning has given me cold feet. It seems that the brand new cruise ship, Sun Empress, has come to grief in a storm off the Azores. No details yet, but it sounds serious.

Tom: The Sun Empress! She must be on her maiden voyage!

Alan: Correct. She's a sister ship of the Sun Queen. You may remember that it was the Queen which turned turtle and sank last year, somewhere in the South Seas. Nearly a hundred passengers were sent to Davey Jones' locker in that calamity. Reports of disasters at sea do take the gilt off the gingerbread, when planning a trip on the briny.

Tom: Oh, I wouldn't say that. Most people'd be tickled pink to go on a cruise. How else can one live in the lap of luxury and see the world at the same time? If everyone felt like you, ocean travel wouldn't be the fast growing industry it is today.

Alan: I see your point, but I still can't help feeling chicken about planning such a risky vacation.

Tom: I'd take the risk any day just to enjoy the food on the ships. Out of this world, isn't it?

Alan: Oh, I agree. Trouble is, the chefs go overboard, especially with the wickedly tempting mid-day smorgasbords. One's eyes become bigger than one's stomach, one overeats, gets indigestion, and has to spend the afternoon recovering in the arms of Morpheus. On our last trip I missed so many after lunch activities that I wondered if the bundle I'd paid for the cruise was really worth it.

Tom: Altogether, it sounds as if a trip to Europe would be more up your alley.

Alan: No thanks! That would mean taking to the air. Crowded airports and jet lag are not our cup of tea. We'll probably scrub the whole idea of a vacation and just stay home. Marilyn would be in her element baby-sitting our new grandchild, and I'd have a shot at improving my golf handicap. I might even toss my hat into the ring when the local summer tournament comes around.

Second Thoughts — Idioms

Golden handshake	Gift presented on the occasion of a long-time employee's retirement
In the cards	A possibility
Be a bad sailor	Gets seasick very easily
Feed the fish	Be seasick
Give it a whirl	Give it a try or a chance
Have cold feet	Be nervous about undertaking what might be a risky happening
Brand new	Used for the first time
Come to grief	Get into bad trouble
Maiden voyage	First trip
Turn turtle	Capsize, turn up-side-down
Sent to Davey Jones' locker	Drowned at sea
To take the gilt off the gingerbread	To spoil something which promises to be good
Tickled pink	Very happy
In the lap of luxury	In great comfort

Feel chicken	Feel nervous, afraid
Out of this world	Wonderful
To go overboard	Go to excess
Have eyes bigger than the stomach	Be greedy for appealing food and so east too much
In the arms of Morpheus	Asleep (Morpheus is the god of sleep)
A bundle	A lot of money
Up his alley	Suited to his personality
Take to the air	Fly in a plane
Not our cup of tea	Not the sort of thing we like
To scrub	To cancel
Be in one's element	Be in a situation one is ideally suited for
Have a shot at	Attempt to do...
Toss hat into ring	Enter a contest or competition

Ripped Off!

Chuck: I'm fed up. You know that new salesman, George, at the used car dealership next to the greasy spoon on Pitt Street?

Uncle: Yes, a tall fellow with a five o'clock shadow.

Chuck: Well, he's just sold me a lemon after swearing that the 1980 Packman I bought was in excellent condition.

Uncle: Bad luck. What's wrong with it?

Chuck: To call a spade a spade, it's a clunker, ready to conk out at every stop light. The windshield wipers are haywire, the brakes shot, and you should see the rust. On top of all that, I've read that the Packman is a hot little car, but this one couldn't pull the skin off a rice pudding.

Uncle: Didn't you get a mechanic to check it over? Take it for a spin around the block? Discuss the possibility of a warranty?

Chuck: I just took George's word that everything was okay. And the colour of the car attracted me — it's the exact shade of purple that my girlfriend is crazy about. Our relationship is a little rocky at the moment and . . .

Uncle: What nonsense you do talk, Chuck. Listen, if you think you've been taken for a ride, take the car back and complain to the sales manager.

Chuck: I suppose I should, but I'm afraid that George would get into hot water for lying about it. I know that he's been

	unemployed for donkey's years. I've walked in his shoes and know how it feels to land a job at last. I'd hate to put a spoke in his wheel when he's only just started working. He might get fired.
Uncle:	I am losing patience with you. George has pulled the wool over your eyes and knowingly sold you a lemon, yet you are ready to take it lying down. You're bonkers. If you refuse to return the car, then stop bitching, waive your losses and swallow your medicine.
Chuck:	But it will be ages before I can afford to buy another car.
Uncle:	Cheer up. You'll be in funds again before long, and wiser too, let's hope. Then I'll recommend a reputable dealership, guaranteed not to hoodwink customers, or break the bank. Remember, it's all very well to be your brother's keeper, but one can go too far and get landed up the creek.

Ripped Off! — Idioms

Greasy spoon	Low class café
Five o'clock shadow	Unshaven look
Lemon	Useless object
Call a spade a spade	Speak the truth
Clunker	Car in very poor condition
Conk out	Stall, break down
Haywire	Out of order
Shot	Broken
Hot car	Powerful car
Can't pull the skin off a rice pudding	Has almost no power
Take for a spin	Try out on the road
Rocky	Shaky, uncertain
Take for a ride	Deceive
Be in hot water	Be in trouble
Donkey's years	A long time
I've walked in his shoes	I've had the same experience

Land a job	Get a job
Put a spoke in his wheel	Spoil his chances
Pull wool over eyes	Cheat
Take it lying down	Accept without complaining
Be in funds	Have money
Hoodwink	Cheat
Break the bank	Cost too much
Brother's keeper	Person who cares for the welfare of others
Up the creek	In trouble

A Sight For The Gods

Diane: I came across Susan in the Mall yesterday, as usual dressed in the height of fashion.

Pam: I don't know how she manages it. I heard that she's having trouble making ends meet now that her rent is almost doubled.

Diane: Well, Susan's very clever with her needle and makes all her outfits. She's been burning the midnight oil for weeks, getting clothes ready for her trip. She's just back from Africa, you know. She went to Zimbabwe.

Pam: Really! How could she afford a trip like that?

Diane: I believe she had a windfall from an aunt.

Pam: Some people have all the luck! No one ever coughed up any money for me. Did she have a good time?

Diane: Oh, she had a whale of a time. She visited a game park *and* was invited to spend a wonderful weekend in Harare.

Pam: However did she come by that invitation?

Diane: It seems that she met a rich and charming African chief. Most men sit up and take notice of a looker like Susan, and the chief was no exception. You could say that she threw him for a loop.

Pam: So it was he who invited her. Did Susan fall for him?

Chatting in Idiomatic English

Diane: Oh yes, she was swept off her feet. Anyway, they drove to Harare in his super sports car and sure whooped it up when they got there.

Pam: I wonder if Susan ever thought about the new boyfriend she'd just started dating. Out of sight, out of mind, I suppose.

Diane: She was probably enjoying her spree too much to think of him.

Pam: Getting home to her little apartment must have been a real let-down.

Diane: Yes, I think she's finding the daily round in the suburbs horribly humdrum.

Pam: Is she planning to return to Africa?

Diane: No. She says there's not a ghost of a chance of doing that. She's consoling herself by making a fabulous new wardrobe out of some gorgeous yard goods she bought in the bazaars. She'll be a sight for the gods at the Gallery reception next week.

A Sight For The Gods — Idioms

Come across	Meet
Height of fashion	Latest fashion
Make ends meet	Have just enough income to live on
Be clever with one's needle	Be good at sewing
Burn the midnight oil	Work late at night
Windfall	Unexpected gift, usually money
Cough up	Produce as a gift
A whale of a time	A wonderful time
Come by	Get, achieve
Sits up and takes notice	Is very interested in and attracted by
A looker	A very attractive woman
Be thrown for a loop	Be overwhelmed
Fall for	Be very attracted to
Be swept off one's feet	Be excited and thrilled
Whoop it up	Party; have a wild time

Start dating	Start to take out, as a boyfriend or a girlfriend
A let-down	An anticlimax
Daily round	Everyday routine
Humdrum	Boring
Not a ghost of a chance	No chance at all
Be a sight for the gods	Be beautiful

Where There's A Will There's A Way

Miss Thom: I'm afraid I'll have to pass up your picnic tomorrow. I have to keep my nose to the grindstone on Saturdays.

Barbara: Can't you tell your boss a white lie and say you were sick on the weekend?

Miss Thom: Oh, I couldn't do that. I'd be called on the carpet if I were found out. Anyway, I find picnics tiring at my age. I have so little energy nowadays.

Barbara: What a pity. I'm sorry you can't make it. Mrs. Dodd is coming. Do you know her?

Miss Thom: Yes. She's nice, but she talks too much. Her endless yakking is exhausting.

Barbara: I know what you mean, but I'm sorry for her. She's very lonely and loves being asked out.

Miss Thom: You are so kind to anyone who's feeling down in the dumps.

Barbara: Well, one good turn deserves another. My little girl is often sick and Mrs. Dodd comes to read to her for hours. It's such a help. Are you sure you can't come?

Miss Thom: I'm afraid so. For one thing, I'm stiff as a board after gardening yesterday.

Barbara: I was in the same boat last week, but just two treatments by a physiotherapist put me right.

Miss Thom: You certainly do look in the pink.

Barbara: *You* should try a physio. Better still, join a health and fitness centre and get into shape. *And* take a stand with your boss — refuse to work on Saturdays. You could have a whole new lease on life. You're not over the hill yet.

Miss Thom: You are right, Barbara. I must take myself in hand. Tomorrow I'll phone the fitness centre and talk to my boss. I just hope I won't get the sack.

Barbara: I'm sure you won't. Your boss thinks he can get away with overworking his employees and will find out that he's mistaken. Come for a picnic with us next month.

Miss Thom: Thank you, and please ask Mrs. Dodd. If the fitness centre comes up to scratch, I should be able to handle her incessant chatter without going around the bend.

Where There's A Will There's A Way — Idioms

To pass up	To be unable to accept an invitation, etc.
Keep one's nose to the grindstone	Keep working hard
White lie	Small, unimportant lie
Be called on the carpet	Be reprimanded
Can't make it	Can't go, or come
Down in the dumps	Depressed
One good turn deserves another	(Meaning is obvious)
Stiff as a board	Very stiff
Be in the same boat	Have the same experience
Fit as a fiddle	Very fit and well
Be in the pink	Very fit and well
Get into shape	Get physically fit
To take a stand	To be firm, make one's position clear
Have a new lease on life	Feel younger and fitter
Not over the hill	Not too old to be capable of work, and enjoyment in life.

Take oneself in hand	Make an effort to improve oneself
Get the sack	Be dismissed
Get away with	Do what one likes without anybody objecting
Come up to scratch	Achieve promised results
To handle	To manage a situation
Go around the bend	Go mad

Father And Son

Tom: Did you know that Wayne Potter's thrown up the clerical job he started recently at a construction company?

Friend: Yes. I heard through the grapevine, and I'm not surprised. Wayne's not cut out for life behind a desk.

Tom: He only took the job to get his father off his back. Mr. Potter's been threatening for months to throw him out of the house and disown him if he didn't get down to work.

Friend: How did a couch potato like Wayne manage to get a job?

Tom: It was offered to him as a favour because his father had helped to get the company out of a serious jam last year. They must have felt put on the spot to do something for the boy in return.

Friend: No wonder Mr. Potter blew his top when Wayne quit, leaving the firm in the lurch. That sort of thing can upset the apple cart in any business at this time of year.

Tom: You should have heard old Potter tearing a strip off Wayne.

Friend: It served him right to get it in the neck. What's he going to do now?

Tom: He says he's going to travel.

Friend: Travel! Well, I suppose he's foot loose and fancy free. What's he going to use for money?

Tom: He says he'll live hand to mouth and off the land. Maybe pick up the odd job. He's got some hare-brained idea that he could collect tourist material for trekking off the beaten track in the Himalayas, and end up working for a travel agency.

Friend: It's a change to hear him considering work, even if it is still in the future.

Tom: Speaking of travel, wasn't Mr. Potter quite a globe trotter himself once?

Friend: Yes, I've heard his tales of hair-raising adventures in India, when he was a young man, like the time he was cornered in a tent by an aggressive cobra.

Tom: Whatever did he do?

Friend: Luckily he'd bought a panga in Africa and was able to give the brute a coup de grâce. Just one of his close calls during his years of travel.

Tom: I believe that he didn't get a proper job until he was even older than Wayne is now. I hope he'll remember that, when his son returns, especially if the boy really does decide to go into the travel business, or whatever.

Friend: I hope so too. His dad will probably welcome him with open arms and let bygones be bygones.

Tom: I believe you're right. Everyone knows old Potter's bark is worse than his bite.

Friend: And that Wayne is really the apple of his eye.

Father And Son — Idioms

Throw up a job	Quit
Through the grapevine	Through a rumour
Be cut out for	Be suited for
Get his father off his back	Stop his father from nagging him
Couch potato	Lazy person always watching television
A jam	Very difficult situation
Be put on the spot	Be morally obligated
Blow his top	Get very angry
Leave in the lurch	Cause inconvenience by leaving
Upset the apple cart	Cause great inconvenience
Tear a strip off	Be very angry with
Serves him right	Gets what he deserves
Get it in the neck	Be severely scolded
Foot loose and fancy free	With no commitments
Live off the land	Eat whatever food can be found in the countryside

Pick up a job	Find a job
Hare-brained	Crazy
Off the beaten track	Where few people travel
Globe trotter	Person who travels the world
Cornered	Trapped
Panga	Curved knife used as a weapon
Coup de grâce	Death blow
Close call	A happening which could have been fatal
Hair-raising	Very scary
Welcome with open arms	(Meaning is obvious)
Let bygones be bygones	Forgive past wrongs
His bark is worse than his bite	He's not as tough as he appears to be
Be the apple of his eye	Be much loved

Throwing In The Towel

Bob: You may be surprised to hear that I'm going to wind up my business and get into another line of work.

Friend: I'm sorry to hear that. I thought your business was a going concern.

Bob: Not anymore. It's on the rocks and I'm getting rid of the whole kit and caboodle. The downturn in the economy has sounded the death knell for small businesses like mine.

Friend: That's sad, but typical of what's going on.

Bob: Yes, there's too much competition from the big guys, and people are not as ready to part with their money as they used to be. Incidentally, our fork-lift went on the blink last week. It costs the earth to have heavy equipment repaired by the service people, so I got old Sam to have a go. It was a mistake.

Friend: Sam! He's nearly eighty, isn't he?

Bob: Yes. I should have known that he was past it. The trouble went from bad to worse after his clumsy work. Now the lift's only fit for the scrap heap.

Friend: Surely that problem isn't a major reason for you to be throwing in the towel.

Bob: It was just the last straw.

Friend: So you've definitely decided to take the plunge! What are you going to do now?

Bob: When I get my feet on the ground I'll take a course in landscaping. Then I'd like to get a gardening job, working close to nature, without the hassle of the dog eat dog life I've been leading. Gardening's not great shakes as far as money goes, but it would keep the wolf from the door.

Friend: How's your wife taking all this?

Bob: Oh, she's a tower of strength. She always sees the light at the end of the tunnel. And she's a great gardener. Working as a couple, I'm sure we'd have no trouble bringing home the bacon... not much maybe, but my wife's very good at managing the purse strings.

Friend: That's a skill she won't need. With all the beautifying of cityscapes and new subdivisions nowadays, you'll have it made.

Bob: Sounds great. I'll take your word for it.

Throwing In The Towel — Idioms

Wind up	Finalize a sale of a business, or end of a project
Line of work	Job, profession
A going concern	A successful business or project
Be on the rocks	Be out of money
Kit and caboodle	Every last item
Sound the death knell	Suggest the end of project (knell is a bell rung at funerals)
Part with	Give away
On the blink	Broken, not working
Cost the earth	Cost a lot of money
Have a go at	Make an attempt
Past it	Too old
Throw in the towel	Give up on a project
Last straw	Final bit of bad luck
Take the plunge	Make an important decision
Have feet on the ground	Be well settled

Dog eat dog	Intensely competitive
Is not great shakes	Does not pay well, is not useful
Keep the wolf from the door	Earn enough to live on
Tower of strength	Very helpful person
Sees light at the end of the tunnel	Is optimistic
Bring home the bacon	Earn a living
Manage the purse strings	Make good (or bad) use of available money
Have it made	Be very successful
I'll take your word for it	I believe you

There's No Accounting For Taste

Jane I've just had a stroke of luck. You know that I've always wanted a lion cub as a pet and have never been able to find one for sale? Well, I just happened to see one advertised in the *Times*. She even had a name, Sophie. Of course I bought her. She's so cute. So now at last I have a lion cub!

Mrs. Jones: Aren't you afraid that when your cub grows up she'll scare the living daylights out of your friends?

Jane: Oh no. My brother, Tom, owns a full-grown lioness he calls Simba. She wouldn't hurt a fly. I admit that she was rather a handful and led Tom quite a dance when she was small, but now she's like an old family pussycat.

Mrs. Jones You mean she's kept as a pet?

Jane: Oh yes. People always jump to the conclusion that lions are dangerous. But not Simba. She's a real scaredy-cat and wouldn't say boo to a goose. She even performs parlour tricks and brings the house down when she roars and growls on command.

Mrs. Jones What a terrifying performance! Tom can count me out on that one. In any case, I'd be on pins and needles if I had to be in a room with a lion. Your brother is living in an ivory tower if he thinks he can trust the animal to socialize with his friends. How do *they* feel?

Jane: They're not worried. Everyone is used to seeing old Simba padding about.

Mrs. Jones Do you really mean to tell me that the brute has the run of the house! Tom must have taken leave of his senses. Who, in his right mind, would trust a lion to be at large in his home?

Jane: Tom doesn't have any problem with Simba. He'd never keep her in a cage.

Mrs. Jones The best place for any wild animal, *I'd* say. It's better to be safe than sorry. What does your husband say about your crazy idea?

Jane: He did turn thumbs down at first, but Sophie's so adorable that he fell in love with her right away, and actually agreed to bring her home.

Mrs. Jones I can only say that I wish you luck. There's no accounting for taste and we'll just have to agree to differ.

There's No Accounting For Taste — Idioms

Stroke of luck	Sudden piece of luck
Scare the living daylights out of	Scare badly
Wouldn't hurt a fly	Is very gentle
Be a handful	Give trouble
Lead a dance	Give a lot of trouble to
Jump to the conclusion	Form too quick an opinion
Scaredy-cat	Person easily scared
Wouldn't say boo to a goose	Would not dare to annoy anybody
Parlour tricks	Humorous acts performed in the home to amuse guests (a parlour is a living room)
Brings the house down	Makes people laugh uproariously
Count me out	Don't include me
Be on pins and needles	Feel very nervous, jittery
To live in an ivory tower	To be sheltered from reality
To have the run of the house	To be free to go anywhere in the house

Taken leave of his senses	Become unthinking, silly
To be in his right mind	To be sane and sensible
Be at large	Be unconfined
To turn thumbs down	To deny a request
There's no accounting for taste	There's no obvious reason for a person's taste
To agree to differ	To decide not to argue

No Huskies For Ted

Fran: Guess what! Ted's soon off on another wild goose chase.

Jim: Another one? You're kidding. What's he up to now?

Fran: Prospecting. Somewhere in the far north. He's joining forces with a so-called prospector who says that he's found a fabulous ore deposit — gold, I think. He wants Ted to help him finish exploring the area and share in the bonanza. And, of course, make a cash input into a prospective mine.

Jim: That's off the wall! What does Ted know about mining! Where is this El Dorado?

Fran: Naturally, the exact location is very hush-hush, but I think it's about five hundred miles, as the crow flies, north of Flin Flon.

Jim: I can't see a city-slicker like Ted surviving under the tough conditions up there... he'll be a fish out of water.

Fran: I told him that, but he turned a deaf ear. You know Ted, he's such a birdbrain. He'd be a smart cookie to forget the whole idea, especially as he doesn't know the prospector from Adam, or even if he's on the level.

Jim: Well, I hope the fellow knows how to live in the northern boondocks. If anything happened to him, Ted'd be up a gum tree and quite unable to fend for himself. Has he got a gun?

Fran: He's getting one. He belongs to an Animal Rights group, you know, and would only shoot if a grizzly were about to attack him.

Jim: Ted may love animals, but he's scared to death of big dogs. You should see him giving a wide berth to German Shepherds.

Fran: Then he'd better think again before joining the prospector who sounds as if he's the type to have sled dogs, probably Huskies. Ted'd soon get the wind up if he thought he might have to live with dogs even more awesome than Shepherds.

Jim: Especially if we laid it on thick about how vicious and aggressive Huskies can be. We could spin him yarns to make his blood run cold.

Fran: Excellent idea. It should be quite enough to put his plans right off the boil.

Jim: Dead on. They'd go down the tube.

Fran: And Ted would tell that prospector to get lost and find another partner.

No Huskies For Ted — Idioms

Wild goose chase	Senseless expedition
Kidding	Joking
Join forces with	Join up with
Bonanza	Riches
Be off the wall	Be amazing, incredible
El Dorado	Mythical country, rich in gold
Hush-hush	Secret
As the crow flies	In a straight line
City slicker	City lover
A fish out of water	A person unsuited to a place or job
Turned a deaf ear	Didn't listen
Birdbrain	Stupid person, idiot
Smart cookie	Sensible person
Doesn't know from Adam	Doesn't know at all, has never met
On the level	Honest

Boondocks	Northern wilderness
Up a gum tree	In trouble
To fend for oneself	To look after oneself
Give a wide berth to	Keep as far away as possible
Get the wind up	Get nervous
Lay it on thick	Exaggerate
Spin yarns	Tell stories
Make his blood run cold	Make him very scared
Go off the boil	Fade away
Be dead on	Be right
Go down the tube	Fail to be completed, as a plan
Get lost	Scram, go away

A Mother And Daughter At Odds

Mrs. Ames: It was a blow when my daughter announced that she's going to marry a sailor. She'll be a grass widow for most of her married life.

Friend: Oh, I wouldn't worry. Remember that absence makes the heart grow fonder.

Mrs. Ames: Well, I think that being alone for months on end is no life for a young woman, and Jean'll be hard up on a sailor's pay.

Friend: Have you talked to her?

Mrs. Ames: Yes, but parents can talk until they're blue in the face and the kids just tune out.

Friend: I'm afraid that's the way it goes nowadays.

Mrs. Ames: What really upsets me is that Jean could have married a fine man, Jack, who fell for her last year. He made good money and Jean would have been on easy street with him. They shacked up for a while, then decided to tie the knot. Everything was hunky dory, set for wedding bells in the spring, but all the plans went up the spout.

Friend: What happened?

Mrs. Ames: Jack was dead set against Jean working, and she refused to be just a housewife. After a big argument about it, she went out and got a job on the graveyard shift down at the docks. That was enough for Jack and I don't blame him.

Friend: So that was where Jean met the sailor?

Mrs. Ames: Yes, his ship was in port having a refit and she ran into him in an all-night café. Love at first sight, she says, and a wedding next month. I wasn't even consulted. Sometimes I feel like washing my hands of her.

Friend: You are too hard on Jean. Every girl loves a sailor. I was sweet on one myself, once. Look on the bright side. Jean will probably have a very happy marriage, with a job to occupy her while her husband's away at sea, and the thrill of having him at home when he's on leave.

Mrs. Ames: But she'll never...

Friend: Do try not to be a worry wart. I'm sure that you'll find everything coming up roses in the long run.

A Mother And Daughter At Odds — Idioms

A blow	A shock
Grass widow	Wife whose husband is temporarily absent
Absence makes the heart grow fonder	(Common expression; meaning is obvious)
Be hard up	Be without quite enough money
Talk until blue in the face	Talk until exhausted
Tunes out	Doesn't listen
Fall for	Be attracted to
Be on easy street	Live in comfort with no money worries
Shack up	Live as an unmarried couple
Tie the knot	Marry
Hunky dory	Just fine
It's all set	It's all arranged
Go up the spout	Come to an end
Dead set against	Firmly opposed to
Run into	Meet

To wash one's hands of	To give up caring about
Be hard on	Be too demanding, angry with
Be sweet on	Be a bit in love with
Worry wart	Person who worries
To come out roses	To end up happily
In the long run	Finally

A Change For The Better

Wife: Phil's been playing hookey from school again and I'm at my wit's end. With your job taking you away so much, I'm the one who has to cope with him. He's becoming a teenage delinquent and I don't seem able to do anything about it.

Husband: Let's face it, you've always been a softy... not nearly strict enough. When Phil misbehaves all he gets is a feeble scolding which just doesn't wash with fourteen year old kids. They have to be given the straight goods. What's the problem, apart from playing hookey?

Wife: Phil's just started hanging around the malls with the wrong crowd. Several of his buddies have been nabbed for vandalism, B and E's, joy riding... you name it. He actually has a twelve year old girlfriend, would you believe it? You know, I think we should send him to a private school.

Husband: A private school! You have to be well heeled for that. Where're the bucks coming from?

Wife: We could run to it if I got a job.

Husband: I thought it was a given that you're not going back to work.

Wife: It wouldn't be for long. Listen, Phil has to get his act together, stop cutting classes, hit the books and knuckle under to discipline. Private school just might be the answer.

Husband: Don't bank on it. Can you see Phil meekly submitting to wearing a preppy uniform and lapping up all the rules? I wish you'd hang loose for a while over his behaviour. I was a holy terror at his age. I even had sticky fingers for coffin nails at the corner store. I was eighteen before I woke up and began to smell the coffee. So it will probably be with Phil, especially with Mike here.

Wife: Mike here?

Husband: Yes, he phoned this morning. He wants to get a job and find an apartment here.

Wife: You mean your kid brother's coming to live near us. Why wait until now to tell me!

Husband: I didn't have a chance, with you yakking away about Phil.

Wife: It's wonderful news. Phil thinks the world of your brother and looks up to him as a big hero. Remember how upset he was when Mike went to live in Australia? That's when his behaviour began to go downhill.

Husband: Well, there's no one better than Mike to turn Phil around. You feeling more cheerful now?

Wife: Oh, yes. Knowing Mike is coming back has taken a big load off my mind.

A Change For The Better — Idioms

Play hookey	Stay away from school or work without permission
Be at one's wit's end	Not knowing what to do, be in despair
Be a softy	Be too soft-hearted
Doesn't wash	Is no good, doesn't work
Give the straight goods	Tell it as it is, make clear
Hang around	Spend idle time in a certain place or with certain people
B and E (Break and Enter)	Forced entry into premises in order to steal
Joy riding	Having fun driving a car without permission
Be well heeled	Be wealthy
Run to it	Afford it
Be a given	Be an understood fact
Get act together	Start proper behaviour
Cut class, meeting, etc.	Avoid attending
Hit the books	Study

Knuckle under	Submit to
Lap up	Accept cheerfully
Hang loose	Relax, stop worrying
Holy terror	Person always in serious trouble; naughty child
To have sticky fingers	To shop-lift, steal small things
Coffin nails	Cigarettes
To wake up and smell the coffee	To realize that the situation is not what it should be
Think the world of	Greatly admire
To go downhill	To get worse, deteriorate
Turn him around	Change his behaviour
To take a load off the mind	To relieve from worry

In The Money

John: I've just seen Gary driving down the highway like a bat out of hell. That's not like him.

Nick: Oh, Gary's very hyper right now. He hardly knows what he's doing.

John: Why's that? What's got into him?

Nick: Haven't you heard? He's just come into a fortune. It was a bolt from the blue and seems to have gone to his head.

John: So old Gary's hit the jackpot! Good for him. His life will be a bowl of cherries from now on.

Nick: Yes, he sure is a lucky fellow. Who knows what he will do now that he's in the money? I suppose some people would blow it all and have a ball.

John: Or do what a friend of mine did. He also struck it rich, played the stock market and nearly lost his shirt.

Nick: Gary's not likely to speculate. He'll probably step up his good works. He's the benevolent type, a real soft touch and generous to a fault. It's put his family in the red more than once. And he'll knock himself out trying to solve everybody's problems.

John: I've heard rumours that some of his solutions are not always very ethical or even strictly legal.

Nick: That's true, but Gary would stop at nothing to give someone a helping hand. I was in the soup myself once... a little matter of double dealing. Gary was a witness in court for me and got me off with his usual gift of the gab. He had to stretch the truth, of course, and there were some raised eyebrows among those in the know.

John: Gary does seem to get his values rather mixed.

Nick: He's a strange mix of two characters... a highly respected pillar of society as a great benefactor, and at the same time an unethical manipulator. All for charity, of course.

John: You make him sound like another Jekyll and Hyde.

Nick: Well at least his heart is in the right place. He'll be able to respond to sob stories with large cash handouts in the future and that'll make him happy.

John: And maybe put an end to some of his shenanigans.

In The Money — Idioms

To drive like a bat out of hell	To speed, drive very fast
A bolt from the blue	A very great surprise
To go to one's head	To make one over-excited
To hit the jackpot	To win a big prize, usually a lottery
Life ... a bowl of cherries	Life full of ease and good fortune
Be in the money	Be wealthy
To blow it all (money)	To spend it all needlessly
To have a ball	To have a wonderful time
To strike it rich	To get rich unexpectedly
To lose one's shirt	To lose all one's money
To step up	To increase
Good works	Help for the disadvantaged
Be a soft touch	Be someone who responds to all appeals for help
In the red	Overdrawn at the bank
To knock oneself out	To overwork oneself

Be in the soup	Be in bad trouble
Double dealing	Using dishonest business practices
Gift of the gab	Ability to talk well and fast
To stretch the truth	Present the truth dishonestly
Raised eyebrows	Questioning or disbelieving look
In the know	Aware of all the facts
Pillar of society	Highly respected person
Jekyll and Hyde	Person with two distinct personalities, as portrayed in the novel *Dr. Jekyll and Mr. Hyde*
Sob story	Story of misfortune told to someone who might be able to help